Dear Mr Asquith

Acknowledgments

Many thanks to the following publications in which some of these poems first appeared:

Cake, The Cannon's Mouth, Dreamcatcher, The Interpreter's House, Iota, The North, Poetry Nottingham, The Ragged Ravem Press Anthology, The Rialto and *South*. 'Dear Mr Asquith' won 2nd prize in the Buxton Poetry Competition 2009. 'Needlewomen' was commended in the English Association Fellows Prize and 'Property' was a runner-up in the 2009 Troubadour Competition.

Dear Mr Asquith
Nina Boyd

Smith/Doorstop Books

Published 2010 by
Smith/Doorstop Books
The Poetry Business
Bank Street Arts
32-40 Bank Street
Sheffield S1 2DS
www.poetrybusiness.co.uk

Copyright © Nina Boyd 2010

ISBN 978-1-906613-21-1

Nina Boyd hereby asserts her moral right to be identified as the author of this book.

British Library Cataloguing-in-Publication Data.
A catalogue record for this book is available from the British Library.

Typeset by XL Publishing Services, Tiverton
Printed by Biddles Ltd., King's Lynn, Norfolk
Cover design by Utter
Cover image courtesy of Corbis Images

Smith/Doorstop Books is a member of Inpress, www.inpressbooks.co.uk. Distributed by Central Books Ltd., 99 Wallis Road, London E9 5LN.

The Poetry Business gratefully acknowledges the help of Arts Council England.

CONTENTS

9	The Dead Lie Underground
10	Pipes
11	Fruit
12	Uncle Tony
13	How to Forget
14	German Lessons
15	Thelma
16	Miriam
17	Miss Ross
18	Sunny Dog
19	The Big Boys' Bumper Annual
20	Last Supper
21	Protanopia
22	First duty
23	Night duty
24	Medical history
25	Desert
26	When the boy ran into her
27	They Batter My Heart
28	All Saints
29	Property
30	Finding a Friend
31	My Mother's Kitchen
32	Cat in the Hearth
33	The Window Cleaner
34	Iris
35	Camping at Whitby
36	The Man in the Next Tent

37 Diagnosis
38 Station Announcer
39 Going to the Shops
40 With Fly
41 Lanterns
42 Pardoned
43 'All I ask is a windy day with the white clouds flying'
44 Eggs
45 Pompeii
46 Going out with Mother

Votes for Women!

47 Dear Mr Asquith
48 Needlewomen
49 The King's Jockey
50 Postal Votes
51 The Rokeby Venus
52 Ethel Smyth
53 The View from Linthwaite
54 The March of a Thousand Women
55 Census Night 1911
56 Self-denial Week
57 Park-spouters
58 Rational Dress
59 Fire-raising
60 Resistance
61 The Cat and Mouse Act
62 Hats off for the Prime Minister!
63 Leaving Home
64 'Baby Suffragette'

for John Bosley

THE DEAD LIE UNDERGROUND

Books nobody read were kept in a basement
thick with Jeyes fluid and dust. Learned journals
stretched back to a time when vicars studied
philology and archaeology; collected birds-eggs,
beetles, butterflies, an abundance of dead things.

The student of Indo-European languages, silent
on the marble steps, hoped to find others struggling
with Grimm's Law and the Great Vowel Shift;
but there was only The Creep in his ex-army trousers
and Make Tea Not War t-shirt, leaning up against
Neuphilologische Mitteilungen as if he could read
her mind. His rodent eyes ran over her.

She knew he lived down there, nested under
hot pipes among mouse-traps and cockroach boxes.
Nobody believed her: until they missed her,
searched for her, found her trussed, dust-dry,
tucked under a shelf of dead languages.

PIPES

Granny's knickers, vast and pink as the Colonies,
reached down to her knees. She'd been in service;
now she sat spread-legged close to her own hearth
where a kettle simmered on a trivet.

Pipes spent his days with his tobacco jar
and memories of dying boys in France.
Each year on her birthday he gave her
a ten shilling note to buy herself a cardigan.
Each morning she emptied his chamberpot.

She died. Pipes moved in with us. He brought
the chamber pot. Mother held it over the bannisters,
but she couldn't let go. He was silent at our table:
things were different; they didn't suit.
When he went home, she took him casseroles.

Smoke lingered in our house for weeks.

FRUIT

Our father prised open the box, drew two-inch nails
from rough-cut wood. Exotic fruits glowed
under layers of straw: all the way from Jo'burg
where we pictured our white-haired cousins
picking crystallised plums from the trees.

Mother stockpiled tangerines and dates
to cheer up the apples stored in our attic,
each wrapped in a single sheet of the *Daily Mail*.
These were meant for Christmas, too;
but we couldn't wait. We knelt
on the sugar-frosted rug and gorged; even Mother.
Dad wouldn't try the apricots and persimmons,
turned up his nose at foreign muck. He bit
into a wrinkled Worcester Pearmain,
scowled from his chair by the wireless.

We were cold and pale because of Mother:
we too could have bared our arms to the African sun
if it weren't for her fear of snakes. Dad never
met her eye. We felt his resentment
as we filled our mouths with mango, litchi, peach;
scoffed our way to the bottom of the box.

UNCLE TONY

Mother said he was a sex-maniac: she'd heard
the bedsprings when we stayed with them
in Scarborough. I don't remember Uncle Tony;
only custard tarts, and my cousin
showing me how to knit.

Then his photo was in the *News of the World*.
Pills and whisky in a double bed with a woman
who had rabbit teeth and wasn't Aunty Joan.
Suicide was a crime in the fifties; they prosecuted
the ones who failed.

Uncle Tony and the rabbit got six weeks in Durham.
They married afterwards. He was a black sheep now.
I never saw him again. I wondered if she was
as pretty as Aunty Joan, who never had a headache,
never touched so much as an aspirin.

HOW TO FORGET

Dad never missed the Black and White Minstrels,
sniggered at the dark side of light entertainment
while I sashayed into St Peter's with Mum,
prayed for boys at Evensong. Sunday night
was fear of Monday chemistry, ox-bow lakes,
French verbs unlearned, the weekly shampoo
and a bath where our lodger left behind a frieze
of hairs, curls that swam at me, trying to get in.

Homework and roast beef are now as much
in my past as limescale and Billy Cotton; but
I can't make Sunday my own, can't dispel
its ordained silence and enjoy late sunshine,
feet up with a dictionary and the Azed crossword.
Oublier: je n'oublie pas, ils ne sont pas oubliés.

GERMAN LESSONS

There were words that made us snigger:
Fuchs and *Vater*. Verbs went to the ends
of sentences, however far away: we waited
and waited, then plonked down a *verloren*.

Our teacher had no fingernails – we didn't
know why, nor why she sighed like a closing door.
She was never angry, never raised her voice;
but we could tell she didn't find *Vater* funny.

Whenever I hear the word *traurig*,
I smell her satin blouse.

THELMA

Thelma came to our school in the middle
of the year with a bag of sweets, the biggest
any of us had ever seen. The whole class
crowded round her. She was twice the size
of the other girls, brown and muscular,
her frizzy hair a wild mane that tossed
and whinnied in the playground. She talked
about dogs and horses and caravans; laughed
when we asked if she lived by the sea.
She was ten, like us, but couldn't read
or write. The sweets didn't make up for that.
We left her to play on her own. Thelma
stood by the railings, holding on,
looking out, looking for a way out.

MIRIAM

She was brought in by the caretaker
after the prayers and hymns. He held
her arm as if she were his prisoner.
She didn't do German with us,
but we heard her whisper with Fräulein
in quick-fire German, saw
that Fräulein held her hand. We wondered
if we should tell. Someone said
there might be a secret number
like Fräulein's on Miriam's arm, but when
we searched her, there wasn't one,
not on any part of her body. She didn't cry
when we stripped her, didn't say anything.
Her underwear was just like ours, bought
by our mothers from her dad's shop
in the covered market. A group of us went
to look. Miriam was behind the counter.
She smiled at us, introduced us
as her friends, though we were only there
to try and see her father's wrist.

MISS ROSS

I hadn't been back in nearly fifty years
but the verb-endings were still in place,
the grammar fixed. My first French teacher
seemed old as the Bastille, her clothes,
lavender and grey, enrobed thinned bones.
It was as if she had already died, the words
all that was left: *parapluies, charmant, il neige
encore*; her brain a repository of holiday snaps,
romance in that mountain village
where she tasted wine for the first time,
but not the last. Miss Ross didn't like my name,
renamed me Geneviève, determined me
to earn it back by remembering *je suis, tu es*,
the chant still there, beseeching her approval.

SUNNY DOG

I remember you speckled with mud, peeling carrots
for soup, tongue asleep on your lower lip. You hummed
eating honey from the jar; sipped scalding tea; cried
at heroism and malice with equal abandon.

That bush you cut back hard is on fire
outside the window, flowers yellow as butter.
I keep your toolshed tidy, oil the shears, water
your bog-garden on days without rain.

Something was better than this: perhaps a woman
with soft hands and pastry cutters, who paints on silk
and never thinks of apologizing; or just a single self:
you always said you had a desert island in you.

He's got a labrador now, Janet said, when she came
for your clothes. You, who were afraid of next-door's poodle.
Sometimes I expect you to bounce through the door
with a sunny dog, a bag of licorice comfits, a smile in your beard.

THE BIG BOYS' BUMPER ANNUAL

His daughter didn't want to fly. Logical Thinking
was taught at her school. She saw the plane,
she saw the sky and demanded proof
that a 747 with her in it would stay up.
Her father was patient, drew diagrams, drew
a crowd of unbelievers prepared to take
their chances for the sake of cheap sunshine.

He was a man who could explain everything:
why boys are bigger than girls;
how to make an origami pig;
the workings of the human heart.

When his wife found him in their bed,
her best friend nestled in his arms,
she threw water on them as if they were dogs.
He could explain everything. He always could.
But she wasn't listening.
She hadn't been listening for years.

LAST SUPPER

We sliced cucumbers, peppers, spring onions
fierce enough to make our eyes smart. And then
you said: *I'm leaving you.* It was too late
to put off our guests; they arrived together,
with flowers and bottles and kisses, praised
the food, our décor, our shiny marriage;
talked about holidays, suggested we all
rent a villa in Italy or the Algarve.

Your brother's wife was dumb, pink-cheeked,
stared at you across the table. I saw it all:
her avoiding me; you taking her children out
for pizzas, planning a trouble-free takeover.
You didn't know I'd always wanted to do
that trick, pull a tablecloth out from under
the crockery and wine glasses. You know now.

PROTANOPIA

Red and green are one to you:
at traffic lights it's glow for green.
A holly-tree's berries are unripe grapes,
its leaves as red as fire-engines
or, to tell the truth, both are
monochrome, a muddy mediocre.

Sartorial indiscretions are the only clue
to your deficiency. You do not aim
for flight, where port and starboard
differentiate forwards from back,
pursuit from a head-on crash.

Not knowing ruby from emerald
your loss is only mine, wishing as I do
that you could see the jewels that pull
fieldfare and thrush to the mountain ash;
distinguish Liverpool from Plymouth Argyle;
play a successful game of Ludo.

Green and red are all the same to you:
a blush the green of nausea,
envy like anger's rubefaction.
You harmonize, adopt a neutral tone.

FIRST DUTY

The uniform itched like new. It didn't fit,
but they called me Nurse.
My first job was to administer theophylline
to a slow-learner with asthma.
I'd come across suppositories, of course.
But how could I tell the child
that pushing something into her rectum
would help her to breathe?
You can't mean it I said to Sister.
But she did. I juggled all the way down the ward,
hoped someone would say
let me do that but they didn't. The girl shouted
get off you cow, and the woman
in the next bed said *She's not a natural, is she?*

NIGHT DUTY

We knitted gloves, five fingers,
4-ply wool on four needles.
The men snored,
except for Peter, six foot six.

Untouched by narcotics
he would stand on his bed,
building up to a fit. The trick
was to get him down before it started.

Damned annoying when you had
a thumb to turn; but leave him,
and he'd wake the lot.
They'd all want something then:

Any chance of a nice cup of tea?
 a slice of buttered toast? As if
we had nothing better to do. As if
a dropped stitch didn't matter.

MEDICAL HISTORY

He grew up on an island, feet webbed
by disposition. A clever child, musical,
looked beyond the heath and standing stones,
found status in a world of scalpels and medicaments,
walked tiled corridors in a shroud.

Accomplishment buoyed him up,
pulled him to the bottom of the sea.
Sometimes he swims out of the crowd,
Mickey Mouse tie and bulging pockets,
head at an angle, attentive
to the prognosis of sea-birds.
A storm drips from his wrack-hung neck.

I am gentle with doctors now, hear
wind-slapped sails in the beat of a heart.

DESERT

He has encountered angels, caravans,
his mother; followed footprints
that brought him back to himself.
An upturned boat shifts to goat-ribs
blasted white. Jaws furrow the sand,
teeth bared in greeting under eyesockets
huge with loss. He lies down by bones,
the stone in his mouth sucked dry;
savours the taste of hot fat; smells
a woman's perfume in the grains
that flay his cheek; sleeps
in the lee of a horned ghost.

WHEN THE BOY RAN INTO HER

she clutched at his sleeve to steady herself.
He punched her, but she hung on;
he punched her again and again to show her,
wriggled out of the faux-leather jacket;
threaded through saplings
to the road at the edge of the wood.

She fell, discovered the bitter taste of mud,
the deathbed smell of wild garlic. Her bleeding
locked her to the ground. Thousands travelled
the road she could hear but not see. A dog
gave her hope, sniffed at her hand, licked
salt from her face; but the nearest human
was a distant whistle. Blackbirds rummaged
the undergrowth with all the noise of rescue.

Cold before dark, listening to the fainter roar
of wheels on tarmac she fell asleep, comforted
by the sweaty tobacco smell of the boy's jacket,
by the knowledge that she held his identity
in her arms, that one day she would be found;
and that one day so would he.

THEY BATTER MY HEART

These strangers pummel me as if I were dear
to them, wrestle a life that would flicker out,
sputtering in a blood-dark room. They strike
my sternum, shout my name, jump on my ribs;
refuse to allow me to vex them with another death.
Yet I am nothing to them: success is not the return
of a friend, a lover, a familiar face (the postman
whose morning grin would be missed; Kim
at the check-out; a leg-weaving cat) – but satisfaction
at a reinstated sinus rhythm, scoring a lucky
one-in-three, so they can say: *I saved a life today.*
The harder I try to die, the more they deny me.
I come back each time to eager sweating faces
that celebrate me like the first goal in a dismal season.

ALL SAINTS

Water rose over the tops of headstones,
lapped at the feet of pedestalled angels,
stood for days. It left behind exhumed bones
brought to the surface as if by sifting worms.
A doctor's yellow femur leaned against a yew;
a nursemaid's ribcage curled like fingers
round a drowned mouse; rich and poor
grinned at the churchyard from greying skulls.

There was no choice: all were reburied
in a single grave, blessed by a cleric
with damp and rotting timbers on his mind.
The soft pates of the babies he baptised
in the rainy weeks that followed were all one;
the same water wetting undistinguished heads.

PROPERTY

He buys a pair of pyjamas,
striped flannelette like an old man's:
a cord round the waist, a gaping fly
to accommodate a catheter.

A nurse fixes a notice
to his bedhead: FAST AFTER MIDNIGHT.
I don't suppose I shall be, he says,
and she smiles.

In the morning they take him down,
braceleted and triple checked.
Flat on his back, he counts
dead flies in the ceiling lights.

He comes round on a bloody sheet,
all pipework and pain. People shout at him
to wake up, then a needle slides
into his buttock to send him back to sleep.

He wakes from a dream in a clean bed
and peach polycotton pyjamas. In the chair
that smells of wee his wife knits
something purple. *Soon be home*, she says.

Ten days later, they give her his things
in a plastic bag: his watch, dentures, wallet;
an Agatha Christie from the library;
a pair of striped pyjamas, never worn.

FINDING A FRIEND

Sand sugars the backs of her legs, damp still
from the scummy water's edge where she failed
to run laughing into the waves. Under a parasol,
the baby punches green air, making people
stop and smile at his naked energy.

Over there, brown bodies crouch. She edges near,
tries to hear their whispers. A boy looks up
with a go-away frown. But she's already gone
to look at a cat on a lead, digging. It won't
be stroked, squirms away from her.

She lies down and shuts her eyes, letting the sun
scald her eyelids, so that when she opens them
she is blind. She turns over, presses her face
into burning sand, turns over and over, a princess
thrown out of a rolled-up carpet,

landing at the feet of a dog, which licks her face.
His breath smells of chicken and wet flannels.
He leans against her, weighty like a friend,
but he cannot stay, barks goodbye, races
towards a whistle, leaving her slimy and panting.

It is cooler here, spiky in the maram grass. Voices
are drowned by the growl of the sea. She looks
for the patch of home, the blanket, even the baby.
She has landed on the moon, where no people live,
and huge birds hover low overhead,

fanning her cooling shoulders as they wait
to peck out her eyes. The hand that folds hers
is firm and warm. A giant blots out
the dropping sun with his smile. She goes
where her friend takes her.

MY MOTHER'S KITCHEN

Out of bounds on Mondays, sorted piles
of shirts and sheets heaped on the floor.
She scowls into a twin-tub that rattles
and tangoes and spits out grey suds. The lino
gets a good clean, oblongs of orange and green
gleam like wet stones. Water seeps under
its curly edge; dead spiders float out;
live ones make a dash for the back of the stove.

Mother's posh sister pushes open the door,
shifts the hot whites out of position.
Is it all right if I put the kettle on? The war
that had raged for forty-five years depends
on moments like this. Mother lifts her red face
to stare at Marjorie's leopard-skin bosom,
painted lips, hair that is definitely dyed.

Avid for tea, Marjorie fails to see
that she is breaching crying-time,
a washing out looked-forward to,
her sister's solitary weekly chore.

CAT IN THE HEARTH

Our morning cat inched towards the fire,
curling up in the cool ashes before dawn.

I raced to school. In the playground brave boys
with cotton-wool ears flew with arms for wings
and buzzing lips, while girls transacted arcane lore
in knots of exclusivity. Left-handed in the yard
I watched and smiled and vainly sought a friend.
Teachers back from war taught by rote and handed out
milk that smelled of sick. We drank
all the knowledge needed to nourish discipline
and fly a patriarchal empire's flag.

I dawdled home, heel against toe,
glad when his bike wasn't there against the wall.
While the cat watched from the windowsill,
I plaited newspaper, laid kindling, ready for Father's match.

In that room, breathing was a crime, disturbing
the peace of the man who was deaf, but heard
what he didn't want to hear. His voice snarls
in my head: *Stop that noise! Stop it!*

THE WINDOW CLEANER

We crouch on sticky lino
breathing Harpic
while his ladders rattle from room to room.
I don't know why we are hiding.
She is afraid, and so am I.

He is always with me.
I follow instructions,
leave money outside on the windowsill.
Eighteen foot tall, gummy beyond the glass
he leers at his tooth fairy.

I wait for him at night,
hugging my purse
as he taps along the wall,
chamois dangling from his belt
a beast paying in kind.

IRIS

She kept her hair in a drawer,
a tail faded to pale pink,
wrapped in yellowed paper.
The dealer refused to buy:
too short, he'd said; too red.

She lost a baby for want of a shilling;
a husband for want of love for the stranger
who came back in uniform, sat in a corner
and frightened the kids. She lost her looks,
her teeth, her patience, and wished
she could lose her ungrateful boys
who showed their offspring a soft touch.

In the afternoons of old age
she slept on her bed under a cat
that dribbled into the bone cup
at the base of her neck.
That's how they found her,
cold under ginger paws
frantically trying to knead
her back into the warmth.

CAMPING AT WHITBY

Theirs was the best, the grandest tent
with windows and a vestibule, a table
where they dined by candlelight on crab
from down the steps. They made themselves
at home as if the canvas walls were solid
Yorkshire stone, laughed at each other's jokes
and tried to hide the edge of envy when they
compared their offspring's gap year jaunts.
We huddled with our ordinary kids,
shared fish and chips, a sleeping bag
with one who'd peed in his, wished
we were at home in bed where we
could whisper secrets, knowing no-one
heard or cared to hear our goodnight kiss.

THE MAN IN THE NEXT TENT

He was in the only pub, so we had to speak. He told us
he was mapping Ardnamurchan for the Ordnance Survey,
who got it substantially wrong in 1924; said
a mouse had got into his tent and eaten his Mars bars.

Getting up in the night for a pee was awkward after that:
now we knew him, we had to go further away
so he wouldn't hear piss hissing on the shingle.

He left suddenly, didn't say goodbye. The place
where he'd slept soon lost its flatness, and the grass
greened again. It was as if he had never been there.

I remember him every time I eat a Mars bar.
If I ever knew his name, I've forgotten it now.

DIAGNOSIS

When he came back she was making pastry,
dropping cold cubes of butter into sifted flour.
He held her, took comfort from comforting her,
looked over her shoulder into the garden
where a cat plucked feathers from a blackbird.
Don't forget the cloves, he said, seeing
the makings of an apple pie.

    She watched him walk away,
floury handprints on the back of his best suit;
heard the armchair creak; rubbed the butter
into the flour, added water, sprinkled the dough
with tears that rolled out as she stood there,
waiting for the world to come upright again.

STATION ANNOUNCER

WE ARE SORRY TO ANNOUNCE
I curse my mother for teaching me
to speak above our station.
THAT THE 16:26 SERVICE TO LIVERPOOL
By the time I started school
it was fixed. The mockery
HAS BEEN CANCELLED. THIS IS DUE
started in the playground
TO A DEATH ON THE LINE AT MARSDEN.
and never stopped. However,
PLEASE REFER TO THE DEPARTURES BOARD
station acoustics demand
FOR FURTHER INFORMATION.
perfect enunciation; and up here in my box
THANK YOU FOR YOUR PATIENCE.
I cannot hear a word they say.

GOING TO THE SHOPS

He set off for the Co-op with a green string bag:
pasta, pears and a Savoy cabbage on a list
scribbled on a torn-open window envelope.

He never came back. The bag hung like a vest
from its shoulder straps on a stunted maple
at the end of the street. He wasn't the type

for another woman, a travelling circus, retirement
on a Costa after a secret life of lucrative crime.
Only his wife knew that he wanted to be alone,

to get away from the tyranny of blocked drains,
children and children's children, bad news,
stray cats, drinks parties, rain. She kept

going to the shops, expected to see him
by the whole nut chocolate; but he must
have found something better.

WITH FLY

In 1987 on the Isle of Wight I bought
six ounces of cashmere yarn from a woman
who had knitted a suit for her husband.
Come out, dear! she trilled into the back room.

He was a dandy in dark-chocolate.
The jacket had herringbone-stitch lapels,
whipped buttonholes and pockets with flaps;
the trousers a zipped fly. I wondered

if he only wore it in the shop; or if he went
to the Working Men's Club carrying his bowls
in a knitting bag; to a church where the vicar's surplice
was of veil-stitch in 3-ply baby wool;

if she had a twisted-rib shroud on the go;
widows weeds worked on eights and tens;
a headstone on order from the monumental mason,
plain with a moss-stitch border.

LANTERNS

In the paddock where we saw you last
a foal with trestle-table legs leans
into its mother's flank.
Wind fans the grass.

I have watched you stroke the back
of a bumble-bee, your finger lenient
as the violet tongue that flicks
a staggering calf.

We haven't seen you since
a drift of lanterns sailed above our heads,
gaudy orange thumbprints
on a mares' tail sky.

You climbed into that night,
waving your hat; leaving behind
the breath of cattle,
earth-bound tethered beasts.

PARDONED

No need to lie about his age;
so many dead or worse they took
whoever came: miner's lung, flat feet,
feeble minds. Nothing prepared him
for mud thigh-deep, rats that chewed
on dead men's boots, the officer
who wept, hugging his knees to his chest.

He ran, looking for fields of harrowed soil,
vistas of wheat where skylarks sang,
sun-baked men with shouldered hoes
and scythes. He found none. Being found
himself, he must be shot: coward, deserter,
an example to those who longed
to go with him that short route out of hell.

Ninety years on they pardon him.
His great-niece brings a photograph
to show them at the ceremony, smiles
from under a hat she last wore at a wedding,
shakes hands with an official who doesn't see
the point after so long, but nods acknowledgement
of something or other; obeying orders.

'ALL I ASK IS A WINDY DAY WITH THE WHITE CLOUDS FLYING'

A sudden gust bangs the breath out of every sound.
Deafened, he sees walls implode, the fall of familiar things:
desk lamps, remote controls, a volley of pens. Then dust.
Plaster, blood and tears brew a death mask.

A still-living child lies across his knees.
Arms pinned he cannot reach her.

He recites the only poem he ever learned,
a wind like a whetted knife, the salt smell of it.

A woman in a green space-suit shines a torch in his face.
Her mouth mimes. Concrete is lifted from his arms, the light
corpse from his knees. Tubed, braced, foil-wrapped, strapped
he is pushed out into arc-lit night.

A woman, wet-faced, turns away,
shakes her head. His luck grieves her.

He tastes air: chilled, a twist of smoke.

EGGS

I am six. The sun is white hot.
They have sent me to the hen run
with a blue china bowl. Mousey
is pecking the dust, away from
the others who peck at her flesh.
They mutter and strut. Mousey
looks up when I unlatch the gate.
I am proud, but afraid of the shit
and the beaks.

They never give me a blue bowl again.
The dog licks up yolk from the path,
and I am sent to my room, where sunshine
has made the windowsill too hot to touch.

POMPEII

Off-shoots drip from a window-ledge spider plant.
I can't ignore the coincidental seven-legged corpse
on the lino, but she doesn't see it, rolling out pastry
for a treacle tart, lips clamped round a Balkan Sobranie.
Beyond the curtain smoke rises over the allotments.

Dad comes in, rattling a match-box, like he does.
"You're dropping ash into your pie", he says.
"Tart", she says round her cig. He's wrong –
the ash hasn't fallen yet; but now I'm forced
to watch it grow and bend under its own weight,
holding my breath, half of me wanting the thrill
of seeing it fall on to the thumb-pressed edge of dough.

And then the phone rings, which hardly ever happens.
She jerks her head. Vesuvius erupts. The spider petrifies.

GOING OUT WITH MOTHER

She can't remember the name
of the pub, or the name
of the village;
but she knows the way.

In the wrong car park
in the wrong village
the seagulls give her a wide berth.

In the wrong pub
in the wrong village
we eat a meal
which she pretends to enjoy.

In this wrong village
dead people sit behind the counters
of charity shops that smell bad,
staring at their hands.

That was nice, wasn't it?
She pities our city life,
the quiet room where we sit
on the white hairs the cat leaves.

VOTES FOR WOMEN!

DEAR MR ASQUITH

She is a gentlewoman with a stone in her handbag,
a bun-sized piece of gabbro worn smooth by the sea,
picked up on the beach at Combe Martin the last time
she saw her father, her mother and brothers and sisters.

There aren't many stones in London streets. This one
is from the mantleshelf in her furnished room, under
the painting of Judith and Holofernes, beside the rag doll
and the poodle with rubies for eyes: a grey warm stone.

It is wrapped in brown paper, tied with string like a parcel
with no address. Nothing is written on the paper,
but they call these packets 'messages'. This one
is for the Prime Minister, because he won't listen.

She gets down from the bus, holding the bag like a baby.
Neatly dressed, with no show, she hopes to look
ordinary so that nobody will notice her until it's over.
She walks through silent streets, excited by fear.

She was never good at throwing: her brothers hardly ever
let her play, and anyway, she was afraid of the cricket ball.
But she manages to smash a pane of glass in the door,
hears it fall on the floor, goes up to look through the hole.

And then she waits for a policeman to come and arrest her,
feeling foolish because she hasn't attracted a crowd. Not
a single person, in fact. A constable comes by at last,
takes his time, trying door handles, peering down cellar steps.

He looks at the ostrich feather curled in her hat, takes her arm,
speaks to her like a father, though he doesn't understand;
guides her towards Cannon Row, where she sees her first
police cell: a bucket, a plank for a bed, stone walls.

NEEDLEWOMEN

At home in Father's drawing room
I was best at drawn thread work:
couldn't get the knack of French knots.
We sewed each day from three to five,
a buzz, a hum, waited for a proposal,
a legacy, knew that some of us
would grow old nursing parents.
Sometimes there was reckless talk:
bicycles, cropped hair and freedom.

In the Holloway workroom, words
were not allowed. We made shirts
for prisoners from cloth so coarse
our fingers bled. Once we sang,
all of us together, and were sent
back to our cells. Work was better,
friendship signalled with eyes, lips, sighs;
notes slipped inside cotton reels. And,
trained for nothing better, we stitched
VOTES FOR WOMEN round every hem.

THE KING'S JOCKEY

Doors and windows sealed.
Gas on. A cushion for his head.

    He's haunted by her face.

Top hats and trilbys crane
to watch the race for the line
as if nobody has run on to the turf.

    He's haunted by her face.

They fall on her. Her hat
bowls across the track.
They wrap her bloody head
in sheets of newspaper.

    He's haunted by her face.

She knows about horses, stands
firm, ready to catch the reins.
She looks into his eyes. They'll say
it was suicide. He can see
that she's too proud for that.

    He's haunted by her face.

POSTAL VOTES

Miss Solomon and Miss McLellan
read the Post Office regulations
and had themselves delivered
by a telegraph messenger boy
to the Prime Minister.
When a Downing Street official
refused to sign for them,
they were returned, intact.

Others were more direct,
dropping into post boxes
paraffin rags and lighted matches,
paint and pitch, bottles of acid
labelled 'Votes for Women'.

The public didn't like it: attacks
on love-letters, seaside postcards,
cheques and share certificates,
anniversary greetings,
were too close to home.

In 1968 Emmeline Pankhurst became
the first woman to be commemorated
on a British postage stamp.

THE ROKEBY VENUS

Men come daily to gape and grunt
at the shameless rump, see no more
than a woman's white buttocks
inviting them in. She is a cipher,
faceless, asking for it.

Cupid's mirror reflects a face.
Not his mother's face; a plain face,
the chaste face of a domestic goddess,
invisible to the arse's
ardent congregation.

Mary stands where the men stand,
gazes at the face of everywoman.
To save her she takes a meat-cleaver
from under her coat, cuts into the myth;
seven wounds in the flawless back.

For this, museums in London
are closed to women. Men keep coming.

ETHEL SMYTH

She insisted, listened
to the music in her blood,
refused food until they let her go
to Leipzig, where she flowered
in symphonies and operas.

And women! How she loved them,
falling again and again. A passion
for Emmeline pulled her the way
she had always been going:
into the Cause. Composition was set aside.

Two years with no music
but breaking glass;
two months in gaol
with a hundred captive birds.

Her *March* became their anthem,
sustenance for the martyrs
waiting in their cells: hungry, thirsty,
marking time.

THE VIEW FROM LINTHWAITE

She swapped Bloomsbury for Black Rock Mills,
Bohemia for a homespun husband, independence
for a censorious knot of sisters-in-law. Talk
among the antimacassars was of laundry starch,
naughty children, impertinent servants.

Florence scorned black-lead and lavender polish.
Embarrassed by the rustle of a gown not plain enough,
she held out hope to a crowd of tiny shawled women:
better wages, and a vote; shoes and good food
for the children; a voice in a man's world.

In the Tolson Museum, ill-lit behind glass,
her banner. The view from Linthwaite in shiny yarns,
caught in longstitch and couched thread embroidery;
purple, green and gold, heathered hillsides, the canal
and smoky mills, a hard-edged landscape worked in silk.

THE MARCH OF A THOUSAND WOMEN

A drum major leads her band, attracts a crowd:
shoppers, businessmen, whistling youths,
hecklers, policemen, a dog that runs up and down,
up and down, barks, growls, tears at trailing hems.

A tidy child in a sailor suit escapes her nurse's hand,
wriggles through legs to watch the pretty ladies
in white frocks, gay sashes, flowers in their hats.
A marcher waves and smiles; Nurse snatches her charge away.

Sunshine warms the wealthy in furs, a few thinly-clad poor:
weavers, spinners, some hardly women yet, worn out
before they've found their stunted adulthood; others are truly old,
eager for change in what's left of their lifetimes.

The procession takes half an hour to pass. At its end,
boys scavenge for a dropped penny, odd gloves, a scarf;
and then it's quiet again, as if they'd never been, as if
a thousand women and their Cause were just a dream.

CENSUS NIGHT 1911

We spent the night in a derelict house,
drummed our heels to frighten the mice.

Wrapped in our coats on the bare floor,
uncounted women, unaccounted for.

When midnight was past we sang in the streets,
frightened the constables, hurried to meet

our leader at Aldwych. (We didn't expect her
to rough it with us, but she wrote on her paper

No vote, no census, and sent it back.) I waltzed
in her arms, giddy with freedom, my name off the list.

No man's property, nobody's wife.

SELF-DENIAL WEEK

Who was that at the door, dear?
        An extraordinary woman, out on her own
        in a big hat and kid gloves; quite genteel.
        Asked for the lady of the house. I told her
        you were busy, and sent her away.
        I see you've nearly finished your work:
        nobody can darn a sock like my own little wife!
And what did she want me for?
        I'm not quite sure. Perhaps I misheard.
        She asked if you would give up
        your little luxuries, and donate
        what they cost to the Cause. Quite absurd!
        I told her, you deserve all your treats;
        but she said you deserve more.
It must have been Miss Quinn. She promised to call
when I met her at a meeting in the King's Hall.
I wish you had asked her in.
        You went to a meeting, without asking me first?
Yes, dear. I often do.
Today we were given collection cards.
I've put you down for tobacco.
All you have to do is give it up for a week,
and hand over the money to me.
        You want to deny me my tobacco?
Yes; it's your turn to go without.
        Well, I'm blessed!
        And what have you ever gone without?

PARK-SPOUTERS

They called each other *darling*,
refused to be searched
or do anything they were told.
In the end, we had to let them
go to their cells as they were,
and they shouted, smashed windows
with hammers hidden in their stockings.
In Chapel they sang their own songs;
at exercise they marched arm in arm.

They were always kind to me.
We weren't allowed to talk to them,
except to give orders; they weren't
to speak at all, but they did, asked
if we were paid the same as the men.
Well, you should be, and that's what we're fighting for.
One of them sent me tickets for a Procession.
I went, and they all crowded round.
I worried about being seen with them,
I might lose my job; but they said:
you can talk to us, darling, now we're not in prison.

RATIONAL DRESS

Solemn men in bespoke suits straddled
comical velocipedes and ordinaries.
Then the safety bicycle was wheeled in,
something a sane person could ride:
alone, at speed, free to breathe fresh air,
unfettered by the company of a man.
Side-saddle couldn't be done: astride
was the only way. To minimize the risk
of accidents, Mrs Bloomer advocated
divided skirts, boneless stays, Dr Jaeger's
sanitary woollen underwear.
Call them what you will, we were in
trousers, and how we loved them!
Our knees fell apart, waists expanded.
It was almost like being a rational man.

FIRE-RAISING

the weight of the fog
of the petrol

the bulk of the mansion
magnified by fog

the impenetrability of the fog
of the thorn hedge

my scratched hands
(I charged the hedge like a bull)

the cobwebs fingering my face
the cotton-wool wick in my hand

the deafening fog
the sound of breaking glass
the smell of damp
of fog following me in
the glug of petrol
the scratch of a match

lost in the fog
the bells of the fire-engines
the looming helmets
You're out late, ladies!

the glow in the sky
in the grate
warm in the police house
the job done

RESISTANCE

They try to break me with slices of chicken,
the fragrance of hot gravy dabbed on my chin.
Then tea, stirred in a thin cup with a musical spoon,
scours my throat with scalding saliva. All the time
they tell me they will have to force me next.

They prise my mouth open with a metal bar
that tears my lips and gums; pour in slime
from a tin mug: milk mixed with Bovril
and beaten egg; pinch my nose to make me swallow.
(When I am strong enough, I spit it into their faces.)

A tube is rammed into my nose by a doctor, a man
with filthy hands who swears at me and tears
at my clothes. Five wardresses hold me down.
One of them is crying. They force me
three times a day, and every time she weeps.

THE CAT AND MOUSE ACT

Suffragettes are shape-shifters,
mistresses of disguise, photographed
at play in the prison yard by detectives
hidden in vans, purring in the dark
over new-fangled lenses.

When they are thin enough the women
are let out by the back door,
whisked away to grow fat again.
Police in warm coats
watch their doors night and day.

A boy, biting into a pippin,
nose buried in his *Union Jack*, jumps
from a cart to walk up the path
and into the house. Out he comes again,
same apple, same comic,

long hair tucked into a cap,
up on to the dray. A mouse
rattling a box of matches.
Set another trap to catch her quick
before she sets your house on fire!

HATS OFF FOR THE PRIME MINISTER!

Three women ambushed the church at Lympne,
struck him with umbrellas as he emerged,
hatless and in a state of grace. On the golf course,
it was Gladstone, the wrong Herbert, who had his cap knocked off.

On the way to Stirling women lay across the road
to slow his car. More emerged from the hedgerows
to jump on the running boards, belabour him with dog whips.
Only his top hat saved him from serious harm.

When a hatchet was thrown into his carriage in Dublin,
his companion was wounded in the ear, though it was claimed
in court that the injury was caused by a hatpin.
Asquith and his Homburg weren't even touched.

It took a War to bring an end to this harassment.
Asquith let others lose their hats in his defence,
and plodded on. After a stroke he died in his nightcap,
the same year that women won the vote.

LEAVING HOME

1910

Her father has given her everything except
an education, her own key, freedom
to choose a future. Flight from the suitors
is simple: a small handbag, a slammed door,
a single ticket. She leaves behind
a trousseau and her stays.

Tomorrow a barber will crop her hair.
She must find work and lodgings,
join like-minded others, march and sing.
She will send a postcard home, hope
that her mother and sisters will see it
before Papa tears it across and across.

Times are changing. Papa loves her,
but cannot see reasons to loosen her chains.

2010

Her father favours education for girls:
young men and their mothers expect
a little learning with the chapatis and childcare.
Obedience is his due; he tells her
how to vote, expects compliance
in the privacy of the booth.

On graduation day she will leave
her shalwar-kameez and dupatta
in the pink wardrobe they bought her
when she was ten. Her jeans and skimpy tops
hang beside her boyfriend's clothes
in the flat they share on stolen afternoons.

Abbu loves her. He simply doesn't understand,
his heart still in a village a hundred years ago.

'BABY SUFFRAGETTE'

Dora Thewlis, 1890–1976

Up against a viaduct eight ranks of terraces
with hedgerow names; Dora's home
a Hawthorne, its windows now reglazed
with mock-Edwardian lilies in pvc frames
that reaffirm its narrowness, mean as a Liberal mind.

She left school at ten to work in the mill;
by sixteen took home a pound each week,
keeping back a shilling for the Cause.
Waved off by her mother she boarded a train
to march on Parliament, to be arrested, kept

away from her friends in a cold cramped cell –
still bigger than the room she shared at home –
six days alone; but that was better than the chaperone
who pushed her into a third-class carriage
without a word or any fellow-feeling.

Her picture in the *Mirror* was made
into a wild-woman postcard: skirt torn open,
screaming, dishevelled in shawl and clogs,
held between well-fed policemen, giants,
their cheeks round, moustaches impassive.

Back in Huddersfield she's quieter, older. Nothing
has changed for Dora. A hundred years pass,
and Hawthorne Terrace is much the same: except
that the woman who hangs out washing in the tiny yard
owes her the vote she can't be bothered to use.